blackbird & company
WRITING DISCOVERY GUIDE

Intro to Composition:

The Essay

VOLUME 2

Write the Descriptive Essay!

by Kimberly Bredberg, MFA
contributing editors, Sara Evans, Tracey Lane

blackbird & company
EDUCATIONAL PRESS

Visit us at
blackbirdandcompany.com
and explore our full range of Discovery guides:

Earlybird Literature & Writing
GRADES K-2

Literature & Writing
GRADES 2-12

Intro to Composition
GRADES 5-12

Exploring Poetry
GRADES 5-12

Research Science
GRADES 5-9

Copyright © 2016 by Blackbird & Company Educational Press.

All rights reserved. No part of this book may be reproduced or utilized in any form or by any electronic or mechanical means, including photocopying, without permission in writing from the publisher except for the use of brief quotations in a book review.

Printed in the U.S.A.

First Printing, 2016

ISBN 978-1-937200-63-3

V1 01 Jan 2016

www.blackbirdandcompany.com

Table of Contents

INTRODUCTION 4

FOR THE TEACHER 6
    Pre-Writing Exercises 6
    Evaluation 7
    Writing Evaluation Rubric 8

FOR THE STUDENT 9
    Introduction 9
    The Writing Process 10
    The Architecture of Good Writing 11
    The Structure of an Essay 12
    The Blueprint – Descriptive Essay 13
    The Model – Descriptive Essay 14

WRITE IT!: THE DESCRIPTIVE ESSAY 17
    Lesson 1 (week 1): Write an Orange 18
    Lesson 1 (week 2): Write an Orange (cont.) 24
    Lesson 2 (week 3): Write a Person 29
    Lesson 2 (week 4): Write a Person (cont.) 35
    Lesson 3 (week 5): Write an Object 40
    Lesson 3 (week 6): Write an Object (cont.) 46
    Lesson 4 (week 7): Write a Photograph 51
    Lesson 4 (week 8): Write a Photograph (cont.) 57
    Lesson 5 (week 9): Write a Room 62
    Lesson 5 (week 10): Write a Room (cont.) 68

NOTES 75

Fill your paper with the breathings of your heart.

– William Wordsworth

Great Essays

Just as no two fingerprints are alike, every author has a distinct writing style. Voice is the fingerprint of an author. Architectural structures are embellished with the voice of the architect. Essays are embellished with the voice of the writer. Blackbird & Company Writing Discovery Guides have been developed with the fundamental belief that great writing begins with great ideas. As young writers develop confidence in their ability to express their ideas, they will recognize and embrace the power of writing.

The purpose of writing is to communicate.
Students will actively engage in the work of transforming a cluster of abstract thoughts into a single big idea. This course teaches them to coherently communicate that idea within a focused structure while drawing the reader into their thoughts. *Activities will emphasize content, process, strategy, mechanical conventions, and style.*

Writing is for a reader.
Everything that is read, was once written by someone who had an idea. An essay can have many purposes, but ultimately it must first engage the reader. Unless the essay engages the reader, its underlying purposes—to instruct, to convince, to convey—will be lost. *Writing directives will guide the writer through the process of crafting words and develop their awareness of audience and purpose.*

Big ideas can be communicated through a range of writing domains, including creative writing. It is vital that students discover and explore the potential of all types. Some writing describes, some narrates, some exposes, and some persuades. Some writing is simply meant to entertain. All writing has the power to inform. *This 10 week course will focus on composing the descriptive and literary essay.*

Great essays have the power to encourage, empower, and enlighten. For this reason essay writing should not just be treated as a mechanical endeavor, but as a pathway for the writer to communicate the depths of the heart and mind.

Take flight!

For the Teacher

TEACH STUDENTS TO WRITE FOR REAL:
Before embarking on any writing adventure with your students, remember to keep at the forefront of your mind that becoming a writer is a lifelong process.

Too often, the student writer's idea is squelched by the daunting task of getting the grammar and mechanics to toe the line. When students are encouraged to value the work of developing an original idea, form follows function and the writer's idea is elevated. Great essays have the power to encourage, empower, and enlighten. For this reason essay writing should not just be treated as a mechanical endeavor, but as a pathway for the writer to communicate the depths of the heart and mind.

So, the question should never be, "How do I teach my students to write?" But, rather, "How can I keep my students inspired to become authentic writers?"

FOLLOWING ARE TIPS TO HELP YOUR STUDENTS DEVELOP A TRADITION OF WRITING ALONG WITH GUIDELINES FOR EVALUATING THEIR WORK.

PRE-WRITING EXERCISES
Pre-writing is the most creative part of the writing process because this is where ideas are born. Often this first step—the *brainstorming* session—is precisely where writers get stuck.

Each week students will ponder and respond to a series of prompts that will challenge them to move ideas from the recesses of their mind to the paper in front of them. They will also explore vocabulary related to the topic at hand to lead them to a deeper understanding of the process. As writers move through these exercises, encourage them to note as many specific details as possible. This will enable them to develop stronger support for their big idea.

Young writers will want to RUSH this step (or skip it altogether!). However, this unit has been designed to guide students through a deliberate pre-writing process that will help them discover the slower, methodical pace that leads to thoughtful and powerful essays. It is a good idea to have your student read all content and prompts aloud to you for the first few weeks to make sure they are understanding the concepts, and how the unit flows and functions.

READ, READ, READ!
Books are great mentors and reading them has a profound effect on a writer's development. Explore the way authors craft language and develop their voice. Lead students on a journey through passages from great stories and you will empower them to discover the wonder of words.

MINE FOR WORDS AND PHRASES
What do you notice about vocabulary? Can a single word make a significant impact? How do writers shape words into phrases? Can a small phrase make a significant impact? How do words and phrases affect the rhythm of writing? How do words and phrases impact what the reader senses? When students connect to language they become confident, imaginative writers who produce coherent and creative essays that are communicated with a distinct voice.

START A WORD COLLECTION
Use a notebook or journal to start a word collection. Words can be found anywhere and everywhere! Challenge students to always be on the lookout for interesting or unknown words and of course, have them look up meanings for ones they don't know. Sometimes a single word can spark a whole idea!

READY, SET... WRITE!
Where do ideas come from? Nothing sparks student pencils more than a timer and a charge, "You have ten minutes to free write...GO" Slamming ideas onto the page often produces little gems that can later be developed and shaped into a meaningful piece of writing. Encourage your students at the end of ten minutes to read what they wrote and to highlight ideas, concepts, phrases, words, anything that stands out to them as intriguing. Encourage them to bundle what they find in an idea book to develop later.

For the Teacher (cont.)

HAND STUDENTS A RED PEN
Rough drafts should only be written with a pencil or blue/black pen. Empower your students to then work through the self-editing process with a red pen before conferencing. Using a strong accent color will make the process from rough draft to final draft easier. You may also want to use a second accent color for any conferencing edits so it is clear who made what changes at what stage.

THE CONFERENCE, TIPS FOR THE EDITOR
Before conferencing with the editor (teacher), the writer (student) should first make self-edits to their rough draft, sweeping the essay for the usual checks—spelling, grammar, and punctuation—while also paying attention to readability, clarity, and creativity. At the end of each essay assignment there is a Student Self-Evaluation form to help with this process.

As an editor, the cardinal rule is to first read the student work as a reader, paying close attention to the flow of content. Ask yourself if the writing is engaging, is it communicating something believable? Do you enjoy what you are reading? Next, read it again as an editor. Ask yourself if the work is working mechanically. Are there bumpy spots where the writing takes you out as a reader? Do you get stuck on choppy sentence fragments? Are you left breathless by endless run-ons? Are there punctuation problems? Do you find the organization of the sub-topics stray?

After these two thorough readings, share your thoughts with the student who will go back into the writing to refine the structure, add flourishes, and incorporate details that will communicate the big idea more coherently and fluidly while maintaining vocal authenticity.

Once the essay is working on a communication level, the editor should do a thorough sweep for mechanical errors such as subject/verb agreement, punctuation, capitalization, spelling, sentence structure, and so on.

EVALUATING STUDENT WRITING
Always keep in mind:

Anyone can teach writing.

Anyone can evaluate an essay.

First and foremost, you have to be a reader.

The writer is an architect. An essay is simply a collection of specific words crafted into phrases, molded into sentences, constructed into paragraphs, and organized by a specific blueprint. Ultimately, the purpose of any writing is to shelter the writer's big idea. And so, the primary work of the editor is to read the essay (multiple times) and then ask:

→ Is the writer communicating a thesis and is it clearly defined?

→ Is the vocabulary powerful and engaging, does it spark striking imagery?

→ Are the details the writer uses to develop the big idea specific and meaningful?

→ Are the sentences well constructed, are they appropriately complex, or are you stumbling on fragments and run-ons?

→ Do the sentences vary in length to create an interesting rhythm?

→ Is the capitalization and punctuation correct?

→ Do the sentences flow into passages according to the blueprint of the essay for the single purpose of sheltering the writer's idea?

At the end of each essay assignment there is a Teacher's Feedback form to help with this process. You may also use the rubric on the next page to aid and inform your assessment.

Once conferencing is complete, the student should type their final draft, incorporating all edits for a clean, polished, ready-to-be-published essay!

Writing Evaluation Rubric

Use this rubric as a guideline when assessing your student's writing:

ACCOMPLISHED

- → Creatively focuses on the topic
- → Uses logical progression of ideas to develop and supports topic with details
- → Varies sentence structure
- → Uses interesting transitions
- → Makes strong word choice
- → Mature understanding of writing conventions

PROFICIENT

- → Focuses on topic and includes adequate support
- → Uses logical progression of ideas to develop and loosely supports topic
- → Some varied sentence structure
- → Transitions are adequate but not creative
- → Word choice is adequate but not creative
- → General understanding of writing conventions

BASIC

- → Topic is addressed, but unclear
- → Lacks logical progression of ideas and support is weak
- → Sentences are stagnant and uninteresting
- → Lack of transitions
- → Average word choice
- → Partial understanding of writing conventions

LIMITED

- → Topic may be mentioned, but not clearly addressed and loosely supported
- → Organization pattern is weak
- → Writing contains sentence fragments and run-ons
- → Poor transitions
- → Poor word choice
- → Definite misunderstanding of writing conventions

POOR

- → Topic is not addressed or clearly supported
- → Organizational pattern is lacking
- → Sentence structure is insufficient
- → Non-existent transitions
- → Weak word choice
- → Frequent errors in basic writing conventions

For the Student

It's true, an essay is a composition of words that communicate a specific idea in a distinct three part structure. But, an essay, most significantly, is your opportunity to weigh out and craft an original idea.

HOW THIS GUIDE IS ORGANIZED

This course is designed with you in mind and is intended to be self-directed, freeing you to authentically and creatively shape your original, big idea.

This introduction will enable you to discover and delight in the process of writing descriptive essays. Each section of this course contains important information and directives that need to be read and studied carefully. Resist the urge to skim! A thorough understanding of this material is crucial to successful descriptive essay writing.

Before You Begin
→ The Writing Process
→ The Architecture of Good Writing
→ Structure of An Essay
→ The Blueprint – Descriptive Essay
→ The Model – Descriptive Essay

Lessons
→ Lesson 1 (weeks. 1+2): Write an Orange
→ Lesson 2 (weeks 3+4): Write a Person
→ Lesson 3 (weeks 5+6): Write an Object
→ Lesson 4 (weeks 7+8): Write a Photograph
→ Lesson 5 (weeks 9+10): Write a Room

Each lesson is designed to be completed over the course of two weeks, spending 2-4 hours per week. During this time you will be exploring the structure, purpose, and potential of the descriptive essay.

WHAT YOU WILL NEED

Have the following resources close at hand as you work through this guide:
→ Dictionary
→ Thesaurus
→ Red pen for editing

The Writing Process

Before they are ever built, architectural structures are first imagined. Materials are gathered and then, through a series of steps, from the foundation up, a structure is built. In writing, the *idea* is first imagined. Words are gathered to be crafted—words into phrases, phrases into sentences, sentences into passages—until at last, an idea is realized.

1. Imagine a big idea.

Brainstorming begins! Make a list, diagram, topic wheel, or outline to help organize your thoughts before you begin writing. **Remember, your ideas are important!**

2. Get your idea on paper.

It's called a rough draft for a reason! Don't worry about being perfect here. **Get your words out of your head and onto the page using a free flow of ideas.** Skip lines during this initial stage in the writing process so you can easily modify your ideas when you revise.

3. Conference, then revise your idea.

Before you get a second opinion, read your work aloud to yourself and then **ask someone else to read it.** See if the content conveys the idea you set out to communicate in a clear and stylish manner. Make sure your voice shines!

4. Proofread your idea.

Now that you've received feedback and made changes, **re-read your writing carefully**, making additional spelling, grammar, and punctuation edits where necessary.

5. Publish your idea.

Remember, your idea is a gift meant to be shared. Type out your polished final draft and share it with someone.

The Architecture of Good Writing

Mechanics is *Structure*

The **mechanics** of writing—punctuation, spelling, and grammar—are the tools you will use to shape words into sentences, to craft rhythm, and to inject meaning that will direct the reader through your written work. **The essay format is the blueprint you will use to frame your big idea.**

Content is *Function*

The **content** of a written work is your big idea. Content might instruct, convince, convey, or entertain, but fundamentally, you must craft the content to capture the attention of the reader. **Content communicates your big idea.**

Voice is *Beauty*

The voice is the individuality of your writing. Language is shaped by the choices you make. No matter what you're writing about your single purpose is to captivate the imagination of the reader. **Voice is the one-of-a-kind fingerprint of the writer.**

The Structure of an Essay

INTRODUCTION

The first paragraph of an essay invites the reader into the writer's big idea. The essay begins with a general statement called the **hook** that *grabs the reader's attention*. The second sentence of your introduction provides **context** and sets the stage for your big idea. The introduction ends with a very important sentence called the **thesis statement** that clearly states the big idea and introduces the three sub-topics you will be using to support it.

BODY

The body of the essay consists of three paragraphs, structured according to a **blueprint**, which will fully develop the **three sub-topics** of the thesis statement and allow the reader to explore the architecture of the writer's big idea.

CONCLUSION

The last paragraph of the essay opens with a sentence that **weaves** the sub-topics together and leads the reader to the next sentence, an **echo** of the thesis statement. The essay ends with a thought provoking sentence called the **twist** that will leave the reader with a memorable snapshot of the writer's big idea.

The Blueprint — Descriptive Essay

This is the "plan" for writing your descriptive essay in thirty sentences. It consists of five paragraphs: an introduction, three body paragraphs, and a conclusion.

P1» INTRODUCTION (3 sentences)
    Hook – *this sentence grabs your reader's attention*
    Context – *this sentence sets the stage for your big idea*
    Thesis Statement – *this sentence introduces the three sub-topics you will use to develop, explore, and prove your big idea in the body paragraphs*

P2» BODY – Sub-Topic #1 (8 sentences)
*This paragraph discusses the **first reason** your big idea matters*

    Opener – *the topic sentence that transitions into your first sub-topic*

    Factual detail #1– *"tell" something about sub-topic #1*
    Sensory detail – *"show" something that expands on factual detail #1*

    Factual detail #2– *"tell" something about sub-topic #1*
    Sensory detail – *"show" something that expands on factual detail #2*

    Factual detail #3– *"tell" something about sub-topic #1*
    Sensory detail – *"show" something that expands on factual detail #3*

    Clincher – *this sentence closes your first body paragraph*

P3» BODY – Sub-Topic #2 (8 sentences)
*This paragraph discusses the **second reason** your big idea matters*

    Opener – *the topic sentence that transitions into your second sub-topic*

    Factual detail #1– *"tell" something about sub-topic #2*
    Sensory detail – *"show" something that expands on factual detail #1*

    Factual detail #2– *"tell" something about sub-topic #2*
    Sensory detail – *"show" something that expands on factual detail #2*

    Factual detail #3– *"tell" something about sub-topic #2*
    Sensory detail – *"show" something that expands on factual detail #3*

    Clincher – *this sentence closes your second body paragraph*

P4» BODY – Sub-Topic #3 (8 sentences)
*This paragraph discusses the **third reason** your big idea matters*

    Opener – *the topic sentence that transitions into your third sub-topic*

    Factual detail #1– *"tell" something about sub-topic #3*
    Sensory detail – *"show" something that expands on factual detail #1*

    Factual detail #2– *"tell" something about sub-topic #3*
    Sensory detail – *"show" something that expands on factual detail #2*

    Factual detail #3– *"tell" something about sub-topic #3*
    Sensory detail – *"show" something that expands on factual detail #3*

    Clincher – *this sentence closes your third body paragraph*

P5» CONCLUSION (3 sentences)
    Weave – *this sentence links the reader back to your big idea*
    Echo – *this sentence reminds the reader of your specific thesis statement*
    Twist – *this sentence leaves your reader with something compelling to think about*

The Model – Descriptive Essay

Read this model descriptive essay in its entirety. You'll notice it consists of five paragraphs that follow the blueprint exactly. On the next page, take note of how each sentence is specifically labeled.

There's Something About Shoes

Shoes make the world go 'round. What are feet without shoes? Although some people may say shoes are frivolity, I believe shoes are able to transform humanity because shoes comfort the wearer, make them run like the wind, and put a stylish spring in their step.

What more can a foot ask for than an old pair of worn in slippers? At the end of a long day and sometimes the beginning of a long weekend, feet ache for comfort. Slippers wrap around our feet like warm blankets. Winter nights call for toasty toes. Just the thought of slipping toes into matted fur tenderly molded for each toe is soothing. Fur lined slippers are the key to keeping feet comfortably warm. With choices ranging from Australian Uggs to Arctic Mukluks, shoes guarantee protection from the elements. Slippers are necessary for keeping weary feet comforted.

A perfect pair of running shoes are like wings for our feet. Feet have the need for speed, but are, by themselves, slow as a tortoise without good quality shoes. Running shoes support our feet and jolt them off the line with a spring onwards down the path. Feet would surely tire in the race set before them without a good running shoe. Our feet cannot speed through rough gravel or chilly sand or burning pavement. Athletic feet especially need protection. Running shoes brace the elements and wear out so feet don't have to. Running shoes are the stuff runs are made of.

Everyone has a favorite pair of signature shoes. Shoes are an extension of individuality. That certain pair will not only mold feet, but will mold to imagination. No matter what, shoes will always put a spring in the step of the individual. A perfect shoe might be patent leather, tie dyed fabric, or fur from Australia. Where would the world be without a ridiculous shoe? From high heels to clunky indestructible boots, shoes can crack a smile without a whisper. Shoes are simply an extension of individuality.

Next time you slip on a shoe think twice about the old fellow. Where would we be without shoes that comfort, support, and make us smile? After all, you know what they say, "If the shoe fits, wear it."

The Model – Descriptive Essay

There's Something About Shoes

P1 » INTRO

HOOK » Shoes make the world go 'round. **CONTEXT »** What are feet without shoes? **THESIS STATEMENT »** Although some people may say shoes are frivolity, I believe shoes are able to transform humanity because shoes comfort the wearer, make them run like the wind, and put a stylish spring in their step.

P2 » BODY

OPENER » What more can a foot ask for than an old pair of worn in slippers? **FACTUAL DETAIL #1 »** At the end of a long day and sometimes the beginning of a long weekend, feet ache for comfort. **SENSORY DETAIL »** Slippers wrap around our feet like warm blankets. **FACTUAL DETAIL #2 »** Winter nights call for toasty toes. **SENSORY DETAIL »** Just the thought of slipping toes into matted fur tenderly molded for each toe is soothing. **FACTUAL DETAIL #3 »** Fur lined slippers are the key to keeping feet comfortably warm. **SENSORY DETAIL »** With choices ranging from Australian Uggs to Arctic Mukluks, shoes guarantee protection from the elements. **CLINCHER »** Slippers are necessary for keeping weary feet comforted.

P3 » BODY

OPENER » A perfect pair of running shoes are like wings for our feet. **FACTUAL DETAIL #1 »** Feet have the need for speed, but are, by themselves, slow as a tortoise without good quality shoes. **SENSORY DETAIL »** Running shoes support our feet and jolt them off the line with a spring onwards down the path. **FACTUAL DETAIL #2 »** Feet would surely tire in the race set before them without a good running shoe. **SENSORY DETAIL »** Our feet cannot speed through rough gravel or chilly sand or burning pavement. **FACTUAL DETAIL #3 »** Athletic feet especially need protection. **SENSORY DETAIL »** Running shoes brace the elements and wear out so feet don't have to. **CLINCHER »** Running shoes are the stuff runs are made of.

P4 » BODY

OPENER » Everyone has a favorite pair of signature shoes. **FACTUAL DETAIL #1 »** Shoes are an extension of individuality. **SENSORY DETAIL »** That certain pair will not only mold feet, but will mold to imagination. **FACTUAL DETAIL #2 »** No matter what, shoes will always put a spring in the step of the individual. **SENSORY DETAIL »** A perfect shoe might be patent leather, tie dyed fabric, or fur from Australia. **FACTUAL DETAIL #3 »** Where would the world be without a ridiculous shoe? **SENSORY DETAIL »** From high heels to clunky indestructible boots, shoes can crack a smile without a whisper. **CLINCHER »** Shoes are simply an extension of individuality.

P5 » CON

WEAVE » Next time you slip on a shoe think twice about the old fellow. **ECHO »** Where would we be without shoes that comfort, support, and make us smile? **TWIST »** After all, you know what they say, "If the shoe fits, wear it."

Write it!

The Descriptive Essay

In the descriptive essay you have an opportunity to explore the potential of language to describe a specific something. Whether you are describing something ordinary like a spoon or something as extraordinary as a sunset, use this opportunity to utilize your active voice in a creative, vivid manner. Describe not only what you see and what you know but also what captures your imagination about the object, person, place, or event you are describing. Remember to use the essay structure to communicate your big idea.

- → Lesson 1 (weeks 1+2): Write an Orange
- → Lesson 2 (weeks 3+4): Write a Person
- → Lesson 3 (weeks 5+6): Write an Object
- → Lesson 4 (weeks 7+8): Write a Photograph
- → Lesson 5 (weeks 9+10): Write a Room

WEEK 1 – Write an Orange

THE ESSAY – VOLUME 2 | **LESSON 1**

Lesson 1: Write an Orange

➡️ **Descriptive essays describe something very specifically using details to spark the reader's senses. You have an opportunity to explore details that make something unique and share your discovery so your audience might experience what you describe.**

Sensory Description Exercise »

Before you begin writing your first descriptive essay work through this senses exercise to help warm up your observation skills.

1. What do you **see** from where you sit? Look up close and far away.

_____

_____

_____

2. What do you **hear**? Listen for loud and soft noises and also for noises you don't usually think of as noise.

_____

_____

_____

3. What can you **touch** from where you sit? Describe textures, shapes, size, etc.

_____

_____

_____

4. Describe the **smells** around you. Smell plants, clothing, food, and objects as well as the air.

_____

_____

_____

5. What can you **taste**? What do you imagine the things you smell, hear, see, etc. taste like?

_____

_____

_____

WEEK 1 – Write an Orange

WRITE THE DESCRIPTIVE ESSAY! | LESSON 1

Now you may begin crafting your first descriptive essay.

Answer the following questions to help you develop your idea:

What makes orange, orange?

Where is orange?

Describe how the color orange affects the senses.

How does the color orange make you feel? Why?

Painter Vincent Van Gogh reminds us that, "There is no blue without yellow and without orange." What are complimentary colors? Do some research. How do these colors interact?

What makes an orange an orange?

Describe an orange in detail remembering to explore the fruit through all of your senses.

WEEK 1 – Write an Orange

THE ESSAY - VOLUME 2 | LESSON 1

Robert Louis Stevenson once said, "And every day when I've been good, I get an orange after food." Is he implying an orange is more than food? If so, what more might an orange be? What do you think he means?

_____
_____
_____

Describe how eating an orange makes you feel.

_____
_____
_____

What stands out the most as you consider an orange that will help you craft a compelling description of the fruit?

_____
_____
_____
_____

Begin to frame your idea:
....

The Thesis Statement »

Begin the process of writing your descriptive essay by first developing a strong **thesis statement**.

> The thesis statement is the sentence that states the big idea of your essay. There are three objectives of a thesis statement:
>
> 1. Your thesis statement communicates the broad topic and the three sub-topics of your essay.
>
> 2. Your thesis statement tells the reader how you will organize your thoughts in the essay.
>
> 3. Your thesis statement assures your reader your thoughtful idea is worth reading because you have a communication plan.

WEEK 1 – Write an Orange

WRITE THE DESCRIPTIVE ESSAY! | LESSON 1

What do you feel is most important to communicate to your audience about this topic?

Brainstorm some potential sub-topics that will support your idea.

Choose three sub-topics to focus on in your essay.

1.
2.
3.

Now craft a thesis statement that introduces the reader to your big idea by communicating these three sub-topics as the focus of your essay. Refer back to the work you have done in *Thinking In Threes* to help you.

Now ask yourself:
- ❏ Have I thought in threes?
- ❏ Is my thesis statement written in parallel form (same grammatical structure)?
- ❏ Is my thesis statement interesting?

WEEK 1 – Write an Orange

THE ESSAY – VOLUME 2 | LESSON 1

The Hook »

Now that you have your **thesis statement** written, develop a dynamic **hook** to start your essay.

> The first sentence of your essay should scream, "Fire!" Not really, but your hook should grab your reader's attention, spark some curiosity, and draw them into your big idea.
>
> Your hook can:
> - » be an exaggeration or make an outrageous statement
> - » be a metaphor or mystery
> - » state a strong fact or staggering statistic
> - » be a famous quotation
> - » ask a poignant question
> - » be a quirky one-sentence anecdote

Write three different hooks that experiment with some of the previous tips.

_____
_____
_____
_____
_____
_____
_____

Choose your favorite hook and refine it.

_____
_____
_____

Now ask yourself:
- ☐ Will my hook grab the reader's attention and spark some curiosity?

WEEK 1 – Write an Orange

WRITE THE DESCRIPTIVE ESSAY! | LESSON 1

Body Paragraphs »

Now that you have a **hook**, a **thesis statement**, and **three sub-topics**, work through this **body paragraph** warm-up exercise. This will help as you begin to craft each of the three body paragraphs in your descriptive essay.

→ **Remember,** begin with **factual details** that **"tell"** the reader about your topic. Then write a sentence providing **specific sensory** details to **"show"** and expand on the information.

Example:
PARAGRAPH OPENER: Light plays an important role in developing the atmosphere of a scene.
FACTUAL (TELL): Imagine, for example, shining a light on the front of a pear and its shadow enlarging.
SENSORY (SHOW): This makes the scene moody, almost frightening.
FACTUAL (TELL): If you shine that same light source on the back of the pear, its shadow will shrink.
SENSORY (SHOW): This makes the scene less intimidating, more inviting.

Now write the **final pair** of sentences and the **clincher**.

FACTUAL (TELL): _____
_____

SENSORY (SHOW): _____
_____

CLINCHER: _____
_____

The Essay »

Now that you have a **hook**, a **thesis statement**, and **three sub-topics**, begin crafting a descriptive essay describing *orange*. Review page 10 and make sure you work through all stages of the writing process.

1. Hand write your **rough draft** on the following pages incorporating all the pre-writing you have done in this lesson.

2. Type your **final draft** with double line spacing and 1-inch margins. Be sure to insert your final draft into this binder following your rough draft.

→ As you work through the process of writing your descriptive essay, ask yourself the following questions frequently:

» **Do I believe what I am writing about?**
» **Am I following the blueprint?**
» **Have I read through each draft of my essay?**

WEEK 2 – Write an Orange

THE ESSAY – VOLUME 2 | **LESSON 1**

Lesson 1: Write an Orange (cont.)

Rough Draft »

Refer to your pre-writing notes and the descriptive essay blueprint on page 13 as you begin your essay. After your rough draft is written, complete the Student Self-Evaluation form to help you edit, revise, and craft a strong final draft.

After you have self-edited, it's time to get a second opinion on your essay. Give your rough draft to someone else and conference with them about how you can better communicate your big idea and improve your voice and mechanics.

WEEK 2 – Write an Orange

Rough Draft, cont. »

WEEK 2 – Write an Orange
THE ESSAY – VOLUME 2 | **LESSON 1**

Student Self-Evaluation

This is your opportunity to **assess your rough draft** and evaluate the voice, content and structure of your essay. An honest and thorough evaluation is an opportunity for you to learn from your own writing and move through the process of revision thoughtfully and productively.

Student Name

Assignment   Date

Checking the Blueprint »

The first step in the self-editing process is to make sure you have followed the blueprint. **Read through your rough draft** and with a red pen, **label each sentence** (hook, context, thesis, etc.) and **check it off** below as you go. If you find sentences are missing, out of order, or need refinement, make these changes. Remember this is why your rough draft is so important.

P1» INTRODUCTION (3 sentences)
❑ Hook   ❑ Context   ❑ Thesis Statement

P2» BODY – Sub-Topic #1 (8 sentences)
❑ Opener
❑ Factual detail #1   ❑ Sensory detail
❑ Factual detail #2   ❑ Sensory detail
❑ Factual detail #3   ❑ Sensory detail
❑ Clincher

P3» BODY – Sub-Topic #2 (8 sentences)
❑ Opener
❑ Factual detail #1   ❑ Sensory detail
❑ Factual detail #2   ❑ Sensory detail
❑ Factual detail #3   ❑ Sensory detail
❑ Clincher

P4» BODY – Sub-Topic #3 (8 sentences)
❑ Opener
❑ Factual detail #1   ❑ Sensory detail
❑ Factual detail #2   ❑ Sensory detail
❑ Factual detail #3   ❑ Sensory detail
❑ Clincher

P5» CONCLUSION (3 sentences)
❑ Weave   ❑ Echo   ❑ Twist

Self-evaluation continued on next page »

WEEK 2 – Write an Orange

WRITE THE DESCRIPTIVE ESSAY! | **LESSON 1**

Now **read your essay a second time** *aloud*. Circle the best assessment of each component and make notes about how you might strengthen your writing.

1. Follows Essay Format Notes:	Excellent	Satisfactory	Needs to Improve
2. Clearly Communicates My Big Idea Notes:	Excellent	Satisfactory	Needs to Improve
3. Hook Grabs Reader's Attention Notes:	Excellent	Satisfactory	Needs to Improve
4. Thesis Statement & Three Sub-Topics Notes:	Excellent	Satisfactory	Needs to Improve
5. Body Paragraph Openers Notes:	Excellent	Satisfactory	Needs to Improve
6. Details Support My Thesis Notes:	Excellent	Satisfactory	Needs to Improve
7. Good Transitions Notes:	Excellent	Satisfactory	Needs to Improve
8. Compelling Twist Notes:	Excellent	Satisfactory	Needs to Improve
9. Overall Readability Notes:	Excellent	Satisfactory	Needs to Improve
10. Interesting Vocabulary Notes:	Excellent	Satisfactory	Needs to Improve
11. Good Mechanics Notes:	Excellent	Satisfactory	Needs to Improve
12. Vocal Creativity Notes:	Excellent	Satisfactory	Needs to Improve

When you have completed this form it is time to write your final draft, incorporating revisions and refinements that have been made through the self-editing and conferencing process.

Type your final draft with double line spacing and 1-inch margins then insert it into your binder »

WEEK 2 – Write an Orange

THE ESSAY – VOLUME 2 | LESSON 1

Teacher's Feedback

Use this form to grade your student's **final draft**. Refer back to pages 6-7 for evaluation guidelines.

Student Name _____ Date _____

Assignment _____

Process (6 points)	POINTS	COMMENTS
Rough (2)	_____	_____
Conference (2)	_____	_____
Final (2)	_____	_____

Mechanics/Appearance (10 points)

Format (Margins, Indentation, Spacing) (2)	_____	_____
Spelling (2)	_____	_____
Grammar (2)	_____	_____
Sentence Structure (Fragments, Run-ons) (2)	_____	_____
Neatness (2)	_____	_____

Content (24 points)

Hook (1)	_____	_____
Context (1)	_____	_____
Thesis Statement (1)	_____	_____
Body Paragraphs on Topic (6)	_____	_____
Supporting Facts & Details (6)	_____	_____
Clear Sequence of Ideas (6)	_____	_____
Weave (1)	_____	_____
Echo (1)	_____	_____
Twist (1)	_____	_____

Style (10 points)

Sentence Variation (2)	_____	_____
Vocal Creativity (2)	_____	_____
Vivid Words – Concrete (2)	_____	_____
Precise Words – Concise (2)	_____	_____
Consistent Tense (2)	_____	_____

TOTAL POINTS: _____ /50   **FINAL GRADE:** _____

Additional Comments _____

_____

WEEK 3 – Write a Person

Lesson 2: Write a Person

→ **Remember:** The descriptive essay describes something very specifically using details to spark the reader's senses. Through this essay you have an opportunity to explore details that make something unique and share your discovery so your audience might experience what you describe.

Use a dictionary to define:

appearance

behavior

Complete the following:

Choose a specific individual you know well to describe.

Describe your relationship to this person.

Describe the person's appearance in detail.

WEEK 3 – Write a Person

Describe the person's behavior in detail:

What makes this individual unique?

What quirks does this person possess?

What behaviors do you find annoying?

What do you find endearing about this person?

List the details you find most intriguing about this individual.

WEEK 3 – Write a Person

WRITE THE DESCRIPTIVE ESSAY! | **LESSON 2**

What stands out the most as you consider this person that will help you craft a compelling description?

_____
_____
_____
_____
_____

Begin to frame your idea:

The Thesis Statement »

Begin the process of writing your descriptive essay by first developing a strong **thesis statement**.

→ The thesis statement is the sentence that states the big idea of your essay. There are three objectives of a thesis statement:

1. **Your thesis statement communicates the broad topic and the three sub-topics of your essay.**

2. **Your thesis statement tells the reader how you will organize your thoughts in the essay.**

3. **Your thesis statement assures your reader your thoughtful idea is worth reading because you have a communication plan.**

What do you feel is most important to communicate to your audience about this topic?

_____
_____
_____

Brainstorm some potential sub-topics that will support your idea.

_____
_____
_____
_____

WEEK 3 – Write a Person

THE ESSAY – VOLUME 2 | **LESSON 2**

Choose three sub-topics to focus on in your essay.

1. _____
2. _____
3. _____

Now craft a thesis statement that introduces the reader to your big idea by communicating these three sub-topics as the focus of your essay. Refer back to the work you have done in *Thinking In Threes* to help you.

_____
_____
_____
_____

Now ask yourself:
❑ Have I thought in threes?
❑ Is my thesis statement written in parallel form (same grammatical structure)?
❑ Is my thesis statement interesting?

The Hook »

Now that you have your **thesis statement** written, develop a dynamic **hook** to start your essay.

> The first sentence of your essay should scream, "Fire!" Not really, but your hook should grab your reader's attention, spark some curiosity, and draw them into your big idea.
>
> Your hook can:
> » be an exaggeration or make an outrageous statement
> » be a metaphor or mystery
> » state a strong fact or staggering statistic
> » be a famous quotation
> » ask a poignant question
> » be a quirky one-sentence anecdote

WEEK 3 – Write a Person

WRITE THE DESCRIPTIVE ESSAY! | LESSON 2

Write three different hooks that experiment with some of the previous tips.

Choose your favorite hook and refine it.

Now ask yourself:
❑ Will my hook grab the reader's attention and spark some curiosity?

Body Paragraphs »

Now that you have a **hook**, a **thesis statement**, and **three sub-topics**, work through this **body paragraph** exercise. This will help as you begin to craft each of the three body paragraphs in your descriptive essay.

➡ **Remember**, begin with **factual details** that **"tell"** the reader about your topic. Then write a sentence providing **specific sensory** details to **"show"** and expand on the information.

Choose one of your three sub-topics from page 32 and outline three pairs of factual and sensory details to support it:

1a. FACTUAL (TELL):

1b. SENSORY (SHOW):

WEEK 3 – Write a Person

THE ESSAY – VOLUME 2 | LESSON 2

2a. FACTUAL (TELL):

2b. SENSORY (SHOW):

3a. FACTUAL (TELL):

3b. SENSORY (SHOW):

The Essay »

Now that you have a **hook**, a **thesis statement**, **three sub-topics**, and one **body paragraph** outlined, begin crafting a descriptive essay describing *a person*. Review page 10 and make sure you work through all stages of the writing process.

1. Hand write your **rough draft** on the following pages incorporating all the pre-writing you have done in this lesson.

2. Type your **final draft** with double line spacing and 1-inch margins. Be sure to insert your final draft into this binder following your rough draft.

> As you work through the process of writing your descriptive essay, ask yourself the following questions frequently:
>
> » Do I believe what I am writing about?
>
> » Am I following the blueprint?
>
> » Have I read through each draft of my essay?

WEEK 4 – Write a Person

WRITE THE DESCRIPTIVE ESSAY! | **LESSON 2**

Lesson 2: Write a Person (cont.)

Rough Draft »

Refer to your pre-writing notes and the descriptive essay blueprint on page 13 as you begin your essay. After your rough draft is written, complete the Student Self-Evaluation form to help you edit, revise, and craft a strong final draft.

After you have self-edited, it's time to get a second opinion on your essay. Give your rough draft to someone else and conference with them about how you can better communicate your big idea and improve your voice and mechanics.

WEEK 4 – Write a Person

Rough Draft, cont. »

WEEK 4 – Write a Person

WRITE THE DESCRIPTIVE ESSAY! | LESSON 2

Student Self-Evaluation

This is your opportunity to **assess your rough draft** and evaluate the voice, content and structure of your essay. An honest and thorough evaluation is an opportunity for you to learn from your own writing and move through the process of revision thoughtfully and productively.

Student Name

Assignment   Date

Checking the Blueprint »

The first step in the self-editing process is to make sure you have followed the blueprint. **Read through your rough draft** and with a red pen, **label each sentence** (hook, context, thesis, etc.) and **check it off** below as you go. If you find sentences are missing, out of order, or need refinement, make these changes. Remember this is why your rough draft is so important.

P1» INTRODUCTION (3 sentences)
- ❏ Hook   ❏ Context   ❏ Thesis Statement

P2» BODY – Sub-Topic #1 (8 sentences)
- ❏ Opener
- ❏ Factual detail #1   ❏ Sensory detail
- ❏ Factual detail #2   ❏ Sensory detail
- ❏ Factual detail #3   ❏ Sensory detail
- ❏ Clincher

P3» BODY – Sub-Topic #2 (8 sentences)
- ❏ Opener
- ❏ Factual detail #1   ❏ Sensory detail
- ❏ Factual detail #2   ❏ Sensory detail
- ❏ Factual detail #3   ❏ Sensory detail
- ❏ Clincher

P4» BODY – Sub-Topic #3 (8 sentences)
- ❏ Opener
- ❏ Factual detail #1   ❏ Sensory detail
- ❏ Factual detail #2   ❏ Sensory detail
- ❏ Factual detail #3   ❏ Sensory detail
- ❏ Clincher

P5» CONCLUSION (3 sentences)
- ❏ Weave   ❏ Echo   ❏ Twist

Self-evaluation continued on next page »

WEEK 4 – Write a Person

THE ESSAY - VOLUME 2 | **LESSON 2**

Now **read your essay a second time** *aloud*. Circle the best assessment of each component and make notes about how you might strengthen your writing.

1. Follows Essay Format Notes:	Excellent	Satisfactory	Needs to Improve
2. Clearly Communicates My Big Idea Notes:	Excellent	Satisfactory	Needs to Improve
3. Hook Grabs Reader's Attention Notes:	Excellent	Satisfactory	Needs to Improve
4. Thesis Statement & Three Sub-Topics Notes:	Excellent	Satisfactory	Needs to Improve
5. Body Paragraph Openers Notes:	Excellent	Satisfactory	Needs to Improve
6. Details Support My Thesis Notes:	Excellent	Satisfactory	Needs to Improve
7. Good Transitions Notes:	Excellent	Satisfactory	Needs to Improve
8. Compelling Twist Notes:	Excellent	Satisfactory	Needs to Improve
9. Overall Readability Notes:	Excellent	Satisfactory	Needs to Improve
10. Interesting Vocabulary Notes:	Excellent	Satisfactory	Needs to Improve
11. Good Mechanics Notes:	Excellent	Satisfactory	Needs to Improve
12. Vocal Creativity Notes:	Excellent	Satisfactory	Needs to Improve

When you have completed this form it is time to write your final draft, incorporating revisions and refinements that have been made through the self-editing and conferencing process.

Type your final draft with double line spacing and 1-inch margins then insert it into your binder »

WEEK 4 – Write a Person

WRITE THE DESCRIPTIVE ESSAY! | LESSON 2

Teacher's Feedback

Use this form to grade your student's **final draft**. Refer back to pages 6-7 for evaluation guidelines.

Student Name _____ Date _____

Assignment _____

Process (6 points)	POINTS	COMMENTS
Rough (2)	_____	_____
Conference (2)	_____	_____
Final (2)	_____	_____

Mechanics/Appearance (10 points)

Format (Margins, Indentation, Spacing) (2)	_____	_____
Spelling (2)	_____	_____
Grammar (2)	_____	_____
Sentence Structure (Fragments, Run-ons) (2)	_____	_____
Neatness (2)	_____	_____

Content (24 points)

Hook (1)	_____	_____
Context (1)	_____	_____
Thesis Statement (1)	_____	_____
Body Paragraphs on Topic (6)	_____	_____
Supporting Facts & Details (6)	_____	_____
Clear Sequence of Ideas (6)	_____	_____
Weave (1)	_____	_____
Echo (1)	_____	_____
Twist (1)	_____	_____

Style (10 points)

Sentence Variation (2)	_____	_____
Vocal Creativity (2)	_____	_____
Vivid Words – Concrete (2)	_____	_____
Precise Words – Concise (2)	_____	_____
Consistent Tense (2)	_____	_____

TOTAL POINTS: _____ /50   **FINAL GRADE:** _____

Additional Comments _____

_____

_____

WEEK 5 – Write an Object

THE ESSAY – VOLUME 2 | **LESSON 3**

Lesson 3: Write an Object

→ Remember, the descriptive essay describes something very specifically using details to spark the reader's senses. Through this essay you have an opportunity to explore details that make something unique and share your discovery so your audience might experience what you describe.

Use a dictionary to define:

light

shadow

atmosphere

Complete the following:

Choose an inanimate object to describe (soccer ball, shoe, remote control, etc.).

Describe the object.

WEEK 5 – Write an Object

WRITE THE DESCRIPTIVE ESSAY! | LESSON 3

List the details you find most intriguing about this object.

Impressionist painter, Claude Monet said, "For me, a landscape does not exist in its own right, since its appearance changes at every moment; but the surrounding atmosphere brings it to life—the light and the air which vary continually. For me, it is only the surrounding atmosphere which gives subjects their true value." What do you think he means?

Place your object in bright sunshine, near a bright lamp, or shine a flashlight directly on the object and observe how the object's features look in direct light.

Now change the surrounding atmosphere by placing the object in a place where very little light exists. You might try placing it beneath a cloth and lifting the cloth so you are observing the object in low light or place the object in a box and lift the lid slightly, peeking at the object in shadow. How do the object's features change in different levels of light?

WEEK 5 – Write an Object

THE ESSAY – VOLUME 2 | LESSON 3

Begin to frame your idea:
....

The Thesis Statement »

Begin the process of writing your descriptive essay by first developing a strong **thesis statement**.

> The thesis statement is the sentence that states the big idea of your essay. There are three objectives of a thesis statement:
>
> 1. Your thesis statement communicates the broad topic and the three sub-topics of your essay.
>
> 2. Your thesis statement tells the reader how you will organize your thoughts in the essay.
>
> 3. Your thesis statement assures your reader your thoughtful idea is worth reading because you have a communication plan.

What do you feel is most important to communicate to your audience about this topic?
_____
_____
_____

Brainstorm some potential sub-topics that will support your idea.
_____
_____
_____
_____

Choose three sub-topics to focus on in your essay.

1. _____
2. _____
3. _____

WEEK 5 – Write an Object

WRITE THE DESCRIPTIVE ESSAY! | LESSON 3

Now craft a thesis statement that introduces the reader to your big idea by communicating these three sub-topics as the focus of your essay. Refer back to the work you have done in *Thinking In Threes* to help you.

_____
_____
_____
_____

Now ask yourself:
- ❏ Have I thought in threes?
- ❏ Is my thesis statement written in parallel form (same grammatical structure)?
- ❏ Is my thesis statement interesting?

The Hook »

Now that you have your **thesis statement** written, develop a dynamic **hook** to start your essay.

> The first sentence of your essay should scream, "Fire!" Not really, but your hook should grab your reader's attention, spark some curiosity, and draw them into your big idea.
>
> Your hook can:
> - » be an exaggeration or make an outrageous statement
> - » be a metaphor or mystery
> - » state a strong fact or staggering statistic
> - » be a famous quotation
> - » ask a poignant question
> - » be a quirky one-sentence anecdote

Write three different hooks that experiment with some of the previous tips.

_____
_____
_____
_____
_____
_____

WEEK 5 – Write an Object

THE ESSAY – VOLUME 2 | LESSON 3

Choose your favorite hook and refine it.

_____
_____
_____

Now ask yourself:
❑ Will my hook grab the reader's attention and spark some curiosity?

Body Paragraphs »

Now that you have a **hook**, a **thesis statement**, and **three sub-topics**, work through this **body paragraph** warm-up exercise. This will help as you begin to craft each of the three body paragraphs in your descriptive essay.

> **Remember**, begin with **factual details** that **"tell"** the reader about your topic. Then write a sentence providing **specific sensory** details to **"show"** and expand on the information.

Choose one of your three sub-topics from page 42 and outline three pairs of factual and sensory details to support it:

1a. FACTUAL (TELL): _____
_____

1b. SENSORY (SHOW): _____
_____

2a. FACTUAL (TELL): _____
_____

2b. SENSORY (SHOW): _____
_____

3a. FACTUAL (TELL): _____
_____

3b. SENSORY (SHOW): _____
_____

WEEK 5 – Write an Object

The Essay »

Now that you have a **hook**, a **thesis statement**, **three sub-topics**, and one **body paragraph** outlined, begin crafting a descriptive essay describing *an object*. Review page 10 and make sure you work through all stages of the writing process.

1. Hand write your **rough draft** on the following pages incorporating all the pre-writing you have done in this lesson.

2. Type your **final draft** with double line spacing and 1-inch margins. Be sure to insert your final draft into this binder following your rough draft.

➡ **As you work through the process of writing your descriptive essay, ask yourself the following questions frequently:**

» **Do I believe what I am writing about?**

» **Am I following the blueprint?**

» **Have I read through each draft of my essay?**

Lesson 3: Write an Object (cont.)

Rough Draft »

Refer to your pre-writing notes and the descriptive essay blueprint on page 13 as you begin your essay. After your rough draft is written, complete the Student Self-Evaluation form to help you edit, revise, and craft a strong final draft.

After you have self-edited, it's time to get a second opinion on your essay. Give your rough draft to someone else and conference with them about how you can better communicate your big idea and improve your voice and mechanics.

WEEK 6 – Write an Object

WRITE THE DESCRIPTIVE ESSAY! | LESSON 3

Rough Draft, cont. »

WEEK 6 – Write an Object

THE ESSAY – VOLUME 2 | LESSON 3

Student Self-Evaluation

This is your opportunity to **assess your rough draft** and evaluate the voice, content and structure of your essay. An honest and thorough evaluation is an opportunity for you to learn from your own writing and move through the process of revision thoughtfully and productively.

Student Name

Assignment   Date

Checking the Blueprint »

The first step in the self-editing process is to make sure you have followed the blueprint. **Read through your rough draft** and with a red pen, **label each sentence** (hook, context, thesis, etc.) and **check it off** below as you go. If you find sentences are missing, out of order, or need refinement, make these changes. Remember this is why your rough draft is so important.

P1» INTRODUCTION (3 sentences)
❏ Hook   ❏ Context   ❏ Thesis Statement

P2» BODY – Sub-Topic #1 (8 sentences)
❏ Opener
❏ Factual detail #1   ❏ Sensory detail
❏ Factual detail #2   ❏ Sensory detail
❏ Factual detail #3   ❏ Sensory detail
❏ Clincher

P3» BODY – Sub-Topic #2 (8 sentences)
❏ Opener
❏ Factual detail #1   ❏ Sensory detail
❏ Factual detail #2   ❏ Sensory detail
❏ Factual detail #3   ❏ Sensory detail
❏ Clincher

P4» BODY – Sub-Topic #3 (8 sentences)
❏ Opener
❏ Factual detail #1   ❏ Sensory detail
❏ Factual detail #2   ❏ Sensory detail
❏ Factual detail #3   ❏ Sensory detail
❏ Clincher

P5» CONCLUSION (3 sentences)
❏ Weave   ❏ Echo   ❏ Twist

Self-evaluation continued on next page »

WEEK 6 – Write an Object

WRITE THE DESCRIPTIVE ESSAY! | LESSON 3

Now **read your essay a second time** *aloud*. Circle the best assessment of each component and make notes about how you might strengthen your writing.

1. Follows Essay Format Notes:	Excellent	Satisfactory	Needs to Improve
2. Clearly Communicates My Big Idea Notes:	Excellent	Satisfactory	Needs to Improve
3. Hook Grabs Reader's Attention Notes:	Excellent	Satisfactory	Needs to Improve
4. Thesis Statement & Three Sub-Topics Notes:	Excellent	Satisfactory	Needs to Improve
5. Body Paragraph Openers Notes:	Excellent	Satisfactory	Needs to Improve
6. Details Support My Thesis Notes:	Excellent	Satisfactory	Needs to Improve
7. Good Transitions Notes:	Excellent	Satisfactory	Needs to Improve
8. Compelling Twist Notes:	Excellent	Satisfactory	Needs to Improve
9. Overall Readability Notes:	Excellent	Satisfactory	Needs to Improve
10. Interesting Vocabulary Notes:	Excellent	Satisfactory	Needs to Improve
11. Good Mechanics Notes:	Excellent	Satisfactory	Needs to Improve
12. Vocal Creativity Notes:	Excellent	Satisfactory	Needs to Improve

When you have completed this form it is time to write your final draft, incorporating revisions and refinements that have been made through the self-editing and conferencing process.

Type your final draft with double line spacing and 1-inch margins then insert it into your binder »

WEEK 6 – Write an Object

THE ESSAY – VOLUME 2 | LESSON 3

Teacher's Feedback

Use this form to grade your student's **final draft**. Refer back to pages 6-7 for evaluation guidelines.

Student Name _____ Date _____

Assignment _____

Process (6 points)	POINTS	COMMENTS
Rough (2)	_____	_____
Conference (2)	_____	_____
Final (2)	_____	_____

Mechanics/Appearance (10 points)

Format (Margins, Indentation, Spacing) (2)	_____	_____
Spelling (2)	_____	_____
Grammar (2)	_____	_____
Sentence Structure (Fragments, Run-ons) (2)	_____	_____
Neatness (2)	_____	_____

Content (24 points)

Hook (1)	_____	_____
Context (1)	_____	_____
Thesis Statement (1)	_____	_____
Body Paragraphs on Topic (6)	_____	_____
Supporting Facts & Details (6)	_____	_____
Clear Sequence of Ideas (6)	_____	_____
Weave (1)	_____	_____
Echo (1)	_____	_____
Twist (1)	_____	_____

Style (10 points)

Sentence Variation (2)	_____	_____
Vocal Creativity (2)	_____	_____
Vivid Words – Concrete (2)	_____	_____
Precise Words – Concise (2)	_____	_____
Consistent Tense (2)	_____	_____

TOTAL POINTS: _____ /50   **FINAL GRADE:** _____

Additional Comments _____
_____
_____

WEEK 7 – Write a Photograph

WRITE THE DESCRIPTIVE ESSAY! | **LESSON 4**

Lesson 4: Write a Photograph

> **Remember, the descriptive essay describes something very specifically using details to spark the reader's senses. Through this essay you have an opportunity to explore details that make something unique and share your discovery so your audience might experience what you describe.**

Use a dictionary to define:

photograph

province

mood

Complete the following:

Choose a photograph to write about. Is the event a landscape, a celebration, a vacation? Name the event three different ways.

Describe the event being photographed. Be sure to describe the details of the event through vivid sensory language.

WEEK 7 – Write a Photograph

THE ESSAY – VOLUME 2 | **LESSON 4**

Describe the mood of the photograph you chose.

Is the photograph color or black and white? If the photograph is printed in color, imagine it in black and white. If it is in black and white, imagine its details in color.

Photographer Dorothea Lange reminds us, "While there is perhaps a province in which the photograph can tell us nothing more than what we see with our own eyes, there is another in which it proves to us how little our eyes permit us to see." What do you think she means?

What stands out the most as you consider this photograph that will help you craft a compelling description?

WEEK 7 – Write a Photograph

WRITE THE DESCRIPTIVE ESSAY! | **LESSON 4**

Begin to frame your idea:

The Thesis Statement »

Begin the process of writing your descriptive essay by first developing a strong **thesis statement**.

> The thesis statement is the sentence that states the big idea of your essay. There are three objectives of a thesis statement:
>
> 1. Your thesis statement communicates the broad topic and the three sub-topics of your essay.
>
> 2. Your thesis statement tells the reader how you will organize your thoughts in the essay.
>
> 3. Your thesis statement assures your reader that your thoughtful idea is worth reading because you have a communication plan.

What do you feel is most important to communicate to your audience about this photograph?

Brainstorm some potential sub-topics that will support your idea.

Choose three sub-topics to focus on in your essay.

1.
2.
3.

WEEK 7 – Write a Photograph

THE ESSAY – VOLUME 2 | LESSON 4

Now craft a thesis statement that introduces the reader to your big idea by communicating these three sub-topics as the focus of your essay. Refer back to the work you have done in *Thinking In Threes* to help you.

_____

_____

_____

_____

Now ask yourself:
- ❏ Have I thought in threes?
- ❏ Is my thesis statement written in parallel form (same grammatical structure)?
- ❏ Is my thesis statement interesting?

The Hook »

Now that you have your **thesis statement** written, develop a dynamic **hook** to start your essay.

> The first sentence of your essay should scream, "Fire!" Not really, but your hook should grab your reader's attention, spark some curiosity, and draw them into your big idea.
>
> **Your hook can:**
> - **» be an exaggeration or make an outrageous statement**
> - **» be a metaphor or mystery**
> - **» state a strong fact or staggering statistic**
> - **» be a famous quotation**
> - **» ask a poignant question**
> - **» be a quirky one-sentence anecdote**

Write three different hooks that experiment with some of the previous tips.

_____

_____

_____

_____

_____

WEEK 7 – Write a Photograph

WRITE THE DESCRIPTIVE ESSAY! | LESSON 4

Choose your favorite hook and refine it.

_____
_____
_____

Now ask yourself:
❑ Will my hook grab the reader's attention and spark some curiosity?

Body Paragraphs »

Now that you have a **hook**, a **thesis statement**, and **three sub-topics**, work through this **body paragraph** warm-up exercise. This will help as you begin to craft each of the three body paragraphs in your descriptive essay.

→ **Remember**, begin with **factual details** that **"tell"** the reader about your topic. Then write a sentence providing **specific sensory** details to **"show"** and expand on the information.

Choose one of your three sub-topics from page 53 and outline three pairs of factual and sensory details to support it:

1a. FACTUAL (TELL):
_____

1b. SENSORY (SHOW):
_____

2a. FACTUAL (TELL):
_____

2b. SENSORY (SHOW):
_____

3a. FACTUAL (TELL):
_____

3b. SENSORY (SHOW):
_____

WEEK 7 – Write a Photograph

THE ESSAY – VOLUME 2 | **LESSON 4**

The Essay »

Now that you have a **hook**, a **thesis statement**, **three sub-topics**, and one **body paragraph** outlined, begin crafting a descriptive essay describing *a photograph*. Review page 10 and make sure you work through all stages of the writing process.

1. Hand write your **rough draft** on the following pages incorporating all the pre-writing you have done in this lesson.

2. Type your **final draft** with double line spacing and 1-inch margins. Be sure to insert your final draft into this binder following your rough draft.

> **As you work through the process of writing your descriptive essay, ask yourself the following questions frequently:**
>
> » **Do I believe what I am writing about?**
>
> » **Am I following the blueprint?**
>
> » **Have I read through each draft of my essay?**

WEEK 8 – Write a Photograph

Lesson 4: Write a Photograph (cont.)

Rough Draft »

Refer to your pre-writing notes and the descriptive essay blueprint on page 13 as you begin your essay. After your rough draft is written, complete the Student Self-Evaluation form to help you edit, revise, and craft a strong final draft.

After you have self-edited, it's time to get a second opinion on your essay. Give your rough draft to someone else and conference with them about how you can better communicate your big idea and improve your voice and mechanics.

WEEK 8 – Write a Photograph

Rough Draft, cont. »

WEEK 8 – Write a Photograph

WRITE THE DESCRIPTIVE ESSAY! | LESSON 4

Student Self-Evaluation

This is your opportunity to **assess your rough draft** and evaluate the voice, content and structure of your essay. An honest and thorough evaluation is an opportunity for you to learn from your own writing and move through the process of revision thoughtfully and productively.

Student Name

Assignment   Date

Checking the Blueprint »

The first step in the self-editing process is to make sure you have followed the blueprint. **Read through your rough draft** and with a red pen, **label each sentence** (hook, context, thesis, etc.) and **check it off** below as you go. If you find sentences are missing, out of order, or need refinement, make these changes. Remember this is why your rough draft is so important.

P1» INTRODUCTION (3 sentences)
- ❏ Hook   ❏ Context   ❏ Thesis Statement

P2» BODY – Sub-Topic #1 (8 sentences)
- ❏ Opener
- ❏ Factual detail #1   ❏ Sensory detail
- ❏ Factual detail #2   ❏ Sensory detail
- ❏ Factual detail #3   ❏ Sensory detail
- ❏ Clincher

P3» BODY – Sub-Topic #2 (8 sentences)
- ❏ Opener
- ❏ Factual detail #1   ❏ Sensory detail
- ❏ Factual detail #2   ❏ Sensory detail
- ❏ Factual detail #3   ❏ Sensory detail
- ❏ Clincher

P4» BODY – Sub-Topic #3 (8 sentences)
- ❏ Opener
- ❏ Factual detail #1   ❏ Sensory detail
- ❏ Factual detail #2   ❏ Sensory detail
- ❏ Factual detail #3   ❏ Sensory detail
- ❏ Clincher

P5» CONCLUSION (3 sentences)
- ❏ Weave   ❏ Echo   ❏ Twist

Self-evaluation continued on next page »

WEEK 8 – Write a Photograph

THE ESSAY – VOLUME 2 | **LESSON 4**

Now **read your essay a second time** *aloud*. Circle the best assessment of each component and make notes about how you might strengthen your writing.

1. Follows Essay Format Notes:	Excellent	Satisfactory	Needs to Improve
2. Clearly Communicates My Big Idea Notes:	Excellent	Satisfactory	Needs to Improve
3. Hook Grabs Reader's Attention Notes:	Excellent	Satisfactory	Needs to Improve
4. Thesis Statement & Three Sub-Topics Notes:	Excellent	Satisfactory	Needs to Improve
5. Body Paragraph Openers Notes:	Excellent	Satisfactory	Needs to Improve
6. Details Support My Thesis Notes:	Excellent	Satisfactory	Needs to Improve
7. Good Transitions Notes:	Excellent	Satisfactory	Needs to Improve
8. Compelling Twist Notes:	Excellent	Satisfactory	Needs to Improve
9. Overall Readability Notes:	Excellent	Satisfactory	Needs to Improve
10. Interesting Vocabulary Notes:	Excellent	Satisfactory	Needs to Improve
11. Good Mechanics Notes:	Excellent	Satisfactory	Needs to Improve
12. Vocal Creativity Notes:	Excellent	Satisfactory	Needs to Improve

When you have completed this form it is time to write your final draft, incorporating revisions and refinements that have been made through the self-editing and conferencing process.

Type your final draft with double line spacing and 1-inch margins then insert it into your binder »

WEEK 8 – Write a Photograph

WRITE THE DESCRIPTIVE ESSAY! | **LESSON 4**

Teacher's Feedback

Use this form to grade your student's **final draft**. Refer back to pages 6-7 for evaluation guidelines.

Student Name _____ Date _____

Assignment _____

Process (6 points)	POINTS	COMMENTS
Rough (2)	_____	_____
Conference (2)	_____	_____
Final (2)	_____	_____

Mechanics/Appearance (10 points)		
Format (Margins, Indentation, Spacing) (2)	_____	_____
Spelling (2)	_____	_____
Grammar (2)	_____	_____
Sentence Structure (Fragments, Run-ons) (2)	_____	_____
Neatness (2)	_____	_____

Content (24 points)		
Hook (1)	_____	_____
Context (1)	_____	_____
Thesis Statement (1)	_____	_____
Body Paragraphs on Topic (6)	_____	_____
Supporting Facts & Details (6)	_____	_____
Clear Sequence of Ideas (6)	_____	_____
Weave (1)	_____	_____
Echo (1)	_____	_____
Twist (1)	_____	_____

Style (10 points)		
Sentence Variation (2)	_____	_____
Vocal Creativity (2)	_____	_____
Vivid Words – Concrete (2)	_____	_____
Precise Words – Concise (2)	_____	_____
Consistent Tense (2)	_____	_____

TOTAL POINTS: _____ /50   **FINAL GRADE:** _____

Additional Comments _____
_____

WEEK 9 – Write a Room

Lesson 5: Write a Room

→ Remember, the descriptive essay describes something very specifically using details to spark the reader's senses. Through this essay you have an opportunity to explore details that make something unique and share your discovery so your audience might experience what you describe.

Use a dictionary to define:

place

pride

order

chaos

Complete the following:

Describe a room in your house. What is the function of this room?

WEEK 9 – Write a Room

WRITE THE DESCRIPTIVE ESSAY! | **LESSON 5**

Describe the room in detail. Be sure to describe the details using vivid sensory language.

On a spectrum where order is at one end and chaos at the other, where would this room fall? Support your answer with details.

Is an ordered room pleasant or disturbing? Explain your answer in detail.

Is a chaotic room pleasant or disturbing? Explain your answer in detail.

Abraham Lincoln said, "I like to see a man proud of the place in which he lives. I like to see a man live so that his place will be proud of him." Are you proud of your room? Do you think your room is proud of you? Why or why not? What would Abraham Lincoln think of your room?

WEEK 9 – Write a Room

THE ESSAY – VOLUME 2 | **LESSON 5**

List the details you find most intriguing about this room:

Begin to frame your idea:

The Thesis Statement »

Begin the process of writing your descriptive essay by first developing a strong **thesis statement**.

> The thesis statement is the sentence that states the big idea of your essay. There are three objectives of a thesis statement:
>
> 1. **Your thesis statement communicates the broad topic and the three sub-topics of your essay.**
>
> 2. **Your thesis statement tells the reader how you will organize your thoughts in the essay.**
>
> 3. **Your thesis statement assures your reader your thoughtful idea is worth reading because you have a communication plan.**

What do you feel is most important to communicate to your audience about this topic?

Brainstorm some potential sub-topics that will support your idea.

WEEK 9 – Write a Room

WRITE THE DESCRIPTIVE ESSAY! | LESSON 5

Choose three sub-topics to focus on in your essay.

1. _____
2. _____
3. _____

Now craft a thesis statement that introduces the reader to your big idea by communicating these three sub-topics as the focus of your essay. Refer back to the work you have done in *Thinking In Threes* to help you.

_____
_____
_____
_____

Now ask yourself:
- ❑ Have I thought in threes?
- ❑ Is my thesis statement written in parallel form (same grammatical structure)?
- ❑ Is my thesis statement interesting?

The Hook »

Now that you have your **thesis statement** written, develop a dynamic **hook** to start your essay.

➡ The first sentence of your essay should scream, "Fire!" Not really, but your hook should grab your reader's attention, spark some curiosity, and draw them into your big idea.

Your hook can:
- » be an exaggeration or make an outrageous statement
- » be a metaphor or mystery
- » state a strong fact or staggering statistic
- » be a famous quotation
- » ask a poignant question
- » be a quirky one-sentence anecdote

WEEK 9 – Write a Room

THE ESSAY – VOLUME 2 | **LESSON 5**

Write three different hooks that experiment with some of the previous tips.

Choose your favorite hook and refine it.

Now ask yourself:
❏ Will my hook grab the reader's attention and spark some curiosity?

Body Paragraphs »

Now that you have a **hook**, a **thesis statement**, and **three sub-topics**, work through this **body paragraph** warm-up exercise. This will help as you begin to craft each of the three body paragraphs in your descriptive essay.

→ **Remember**, begin with **factual details** that **"tell"** the reader about your topic. Then write a sentence providing **specific sensory** details to **"show"** and expand on the information.

Choose one of your three sub-topics from page 65 and outline three pairs of factual and sensory details to support it:

1a. FACTUAL (TELL):

1b. SENSORY (SHOW):

WEEK 9 – Write a Room

WRITE THE DESCRIPTIVE ESSAY! | LESSON 5

2a. FACTUAL (TELL):

2b. SENSORY (SHOW):

3a. FACTUAL (TELL):

3b. SENSORY (SHOW):

The Essay »

Now that you have a **hook**, a **thesis statement**, **three sub-topics**, and one **body paragraph** outlined, begin crafting a descriptive essay describing *a room*. Review page 10 and make sure you work through all stages of the writing process.

1. Hand write your **rough draft** on the following pages incorporating all the pre-writing you have done in this lesson.

2. Type your **final draft** with double line spacing and 1-inch margins. Be sure to insert your final draft into this binder following your rough draft.

→ As you work through the process of writing your descriptive essay, ask yourself the following questions frequently:

» Do I believe what I am writing about?

» Am I following the blueprint?

» Have I read through each draft of my essay?

WEEK 10 – Write a Room

Lesson 5: Write a Room (cont.)

Rough Draft »

Refer to your pre-writing notes and the descriptive essay blueprint on page 13 as you begin your essay. After your rough draft is written, complete the Student Self-Evaluation form to help you edit, revise, and craft a strong final draft.

After you have self-edited, it's time to get a second opinion on your essay. Give your rough draft to someone else and conference with them about how you can better communicate your big idea and improve your voice and mechanics.

WEEK 10 – Write a Room

WRITE THE DESCRIPTIVE ESSAY! | **LESSON 5**

Rough Draft, cont. »

WEEK 10 – Write a Room

THE ESSAY – VOLUME 2 | LESSON 5

Student Self-Evaluation

This is your opportunity to **assess your rough draft** and evaluate the voice, content and structure of your essay. An honest and thorough evaluation is an opportunity for you to learn from your own writing and move through the process of revision thoughtfully and productively.

Student Name _____

Assignment _____ Date _____

Checking the Blueprint »

The first step in the self-editing process is to make sure you have followed the blueprint. **Read through your rough draft** and with a red pen, **label each sentence** (hook, context, thesis, etc.) and **check it off** below as you go. If you find sentences are missing, out of order, or need refinement, make these changes. Remember this is why your rough draft is so important.

P1» INTRODUCTION (3 sentences)
- ❏ Hook
- ❏ Context
- ❏ Thesis Statement

P2» BODY – Sub-Topic #1 (8 sentences)
- ❏ Opener
- ❏ Factual detail #1   ❏ Sensory detail
- ❏ Factual detail #2   ❏ Sensory detail
- ❏ Factual detail #3   ❏ Sensory detail
- ❏ Clincher

P3» BODY – Sub-Topic #2 (8 sentences)
- ❏ Opener
- ❏ Factual detail #1   ❏ Sensory detail
- ❏ Factual detail #2   ❏ Sensory detail
- ❏ Factual detail #3   ❏ Sensory detail
- ❏ Clincher

P4» BODY – Sub-Topic #3 (8 sentences)
- ❏ Opener
- ❏ Factual detail #1   ❏ Sensory detail
- ❏ Factual detail #2   ❏ Sensory detail
- ❏ Factual detail #3   ❏ Sensory detail
- ❏ Clincher

P5» CONCLUSION (3 sentences)
- ❏ Weave   ❏ Echo   ❏ Twist

Self-evaluation continued on next page »

WEEK 10 – Write a Room

WRITE THE DESCRIPTIVE ESSAY! | **LESSON 5**

Now **read your essay a second time** *aloud*. Circle the best assessment of each component and make notes about how you might strengthen your writing.

1. Follows Essay Format Notes:	Excellent	Satisfactory	Needs to Improve
2. Clearly Communicates My Big Idea Notes:	Excellent	Satisfactory	Needs to Improve
3. Hook Grabs Reader's Attention Notes:	Excellent	Satisfactory	Needs to Improve
4. Thesis Statement & Three Sub-Topics Notes:	Excellent	Satisfactory	Needs to Improve
5. Body Paragraph Openers Notes:	Excellent	Satisfactory	Needs to Improve
6. Details Support My Thesis Notes:	Excellent	Satisfactory	Needs to Improve
7. Good Transitions Notes:	Excellent	Satisfactory	Needs to Improve
8. Compelling Twist Notes:	Excellent	Satisfactory	Needs to Improve
9. Overall Readability Notes:	Excellent	Satisfactory	Needs to Improve
10. Interesting Vocabulary Notes:	Excellent	Satisfactory	Needs to Improve
11. Good Mechanics Notes:	Excellent	Satisfactory	Needs to Improve
12. Vocal Creativity Notes:	Excellent	Satisfactory	Needs to Improve

When you have completed this form it is time to write your final draft, incorporating revisions and refinements that have been made through the self-editing and conferencing process.

Type your final draft with double line spacing and 1-inch margins then insert it into your binder »

WEEK 10 – Write a Room

THE ESSAY – VOLUME 2 | **LESSON 5**

Teacher's Feedback

Use this form to grade your student's **final draft**. Refer back to pages 6-7 for evaluation guidelines.

Student Name _____ Date _____

Assignment _____

	POINTS	COMMENTS
Process (6 points)		
Rough (2)	_____	_____
Conference (2)	_____	_____
Final (2)	_____	_____
Mechanics/Appearance (10 points)		
Format (Margins, Indentation, Spacing) (2)	_____	_____
Spelling (2)	_____	_____
Grammar (2)	_____	_____
Sentence Structure (Fragments, Run-ons) (2)	_____	_____
Neatness (2)	_____	_____
Content (24 points)		
Hook (1)	_____	_____
Context (1)	_____	_____
Thesis Statement (1)	_____	_____
Body Paragraphs on Topic (6)	_____	_____
Supporting Facts & Details (6)	_____	_____
Clear Sequence of Ideas (6)	_____	_____
Weave (1)	_____	_____
Echo (1)	_____	_____
Twist (1)	_____	_____
Style (10 points)		
Sentence Variation (2)	_____	_____
Vocal Creativity (2)	_____	_____
Vivid Words – Concrete (2)	_____	_____
Precise Words – Concise (2)	_____	_____
Consistent Tense (2)	_____	_____

TOTAL POINTS: _____ /50   **FINAL GRADE:** _____

Additional Comments _____

_____

Notes

Notes

Notes

Notes